Happy
Valentine's Day
Love
Mommy '65

For _____

From _____

MAIL-ME BOOKS

BENNETT CERF'S
LITTLE RIDDLE
BOOK

ILLUSTRATED BY

Roy McKie

RANDOM HOUSE   NEW YORK

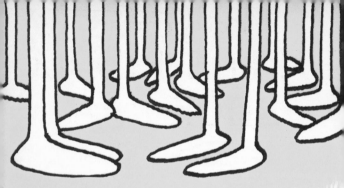

Q. What has eighteen legs and catches flies?

A. A baseball team.

Q. How can you avoid falling hair?
A. Jump out of the way.

Q. Why does a baby pig eat so much?
A. To make a hog of himself.

Q. What is the difference between a tuna fish and a
piano?

A. You can't tune a fish.

Q. Why is a traffic cop the strongest man in the world?

A. Because he can hold up a ten-ton truck with one hand.

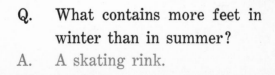

Q. What contains more feet in winter than in summer?

A. A skating rink.

Q. What did the big toe say to
the little toe?

A. "Don't look now, but there's
a heel following us."

Q. Which is faster: heat or cold?

A. Heat. You can catch cold.

Q. What should you do if you catch a dog eating your desk dictionary?

A. Take the words right out of his mouth.

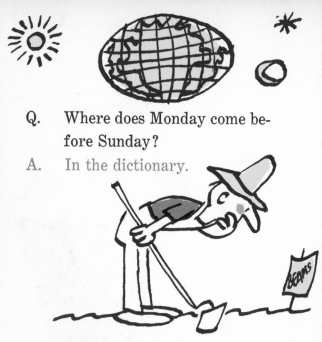

Q. Where does Monday come before Sunday?

A. In the dictionary.

Q. What are the hardest kind of beans to raise on a farm?

A. Jelly beans.

Q. What word is always pronounced wrong?

A. Wrong.

Q. If an athlete gets athlete's foot, what does an astronaut get?

A. Missile toe.

Q. What word becomes shorter when a syllable is added to it?

A. The word short.

Q. When should a baker quit making doughnuts?

A. When he gets sick of the hole business.

Q. What do giraffes have that no other animal has?

A. Little giraffes.

Q. On what day of the year do women talk least?

A. On the shortest day of the year.

Q.   What did the duck say when it laid a square egg?

A.   "Ouch!"

Q. If ten birds were sitting on a telegraph wire and you shot one, how many would be left?

A. None. The others would all fly away.

Q. How can you keep fish from smelling?

A. Cut off their noses.

Q. What happens when you cross a bulldog with a Plymouth Rock hen?

A. The hen lays pooched eggs.

Q. How can you find a lost rabbit?

A. Make a noise like a carrot.

Q. Why did Robin Hood rob only the rich?

A. Because the poor had no money.

Q. Why do birds fly South?

A. Because it's too far to walk.

Q. Where was the Declaration of Independence signed?

A. At the bottom.

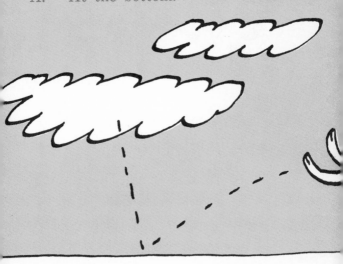

Q. What animal drops from the clouds?

A. The rain, dear.

Q. When Brutus asked Caesar, "How many hot dogs did you eat at the Forum today?" what did Caesar answer?

A. "Et tu, Brute."

Q. How can you make pants last?
A. Make the coats and vests first.

Q. What's the easiest way to double your money?
A. Fold it.

Q. Why is it useless to send a letter to Washington today?
A. Because he died in 1799.

Q. How do you make anti-freeze?

A. Take away her pajamas.

Q. What do people in Hollywood call young gray cats?
A. Kittens.

Q. Why do some monkeys sell
potato chips?

A. Because they're chip monks.

Q. What did the duckling say
when he saw his first colored
Easter egg?

A. "Ooh, look at the orange
marmalade."

Q. How can you know when it's raining cats and dogs?

A. Step into a poodle.

Q. What should a man know before trying to teach a dog?

A. More than the dog.

Q. What did the near-sighted porcupine say when it backed into a cactus?

A. "Pardon me, honey."

Q. What's the longest word in the dictionary?

A. Smiles. (There's a mile between the first and the last letter.)

Q. Why did the moth eat the rug?

A. To see the floor show.

Q. What question can **never** be answered "Yes"?

A. "Are you asleep?"